PLUTO

NEPTUNE

To children's librarians everywhere, but
especially to Mari Martin, Shirley Morrison,
Janice Rorick, and Judy Savage —E.J.

To Olivia, Owen, and Luca—R.M.

Text copyright © 2007 by Ellen Jackson

Illustrations copyright © 2007 by Ron Miller

Millbrook Press, Inc.
A division of Lerner Publishing Group
241 First Avenue North
Minneapolis, Minnesota 55401 U.S.A.

Website address: www.lernerbooks.com

Library of Congress Cataloging-in-Publication Data

Jackson, Ellen B., 1943–
    Worlds around us : a space voyage / by Ellen Jackson ; illustrated by Ron Miller.
        p.   cm.
    Includes bibliographical references and index.
    ISBN-13: 978–0–7613–3405–7 (lib. bdg. : alk. paper)
    ISBN-10: 0–7613–3405–X (lib. bdg. : alk. paper)
    1. Solar system—Juvenile literature. 2. Interplanetary voyages—Juvenile literature.
    I. Miller, Ron, 1947- ill. II. Title.
    QB501.3.J33 2007
    523.2—dc22   2005011058

Manufactured in the United States of America
1 2 3 4 5 6 – JR – 12 11 10 09 08 07

THE WORLDS AROUND US

A Space Voyage

Ellen Jackson

Illustrated by Ron Miller

M Millbrook Press • Minneapolis

CONTENTS

Hi, Kids!

My name is Jason, and I'm 11 years old. I'm getting ready for an exciting adventure, and I'd like you to come too.

As you know, Earth is the planet we all call home. But Earth has neighbors. Our solar system consists of nine planets and more than 100 moons.

Maybe somewhere there's another world with green meadows, gentle breezes, and turquoise water sparkling in the sun. Wouldn't it be fun to find it?

Here's the plan: We'll visit most of the planets and some of the moons. We have a pressurized spaceship, a radiation shield, and a space-warp drive. There's plenty of air, food, and water. Lightweight space suits will protect us from the most extreme temperatures.

So let's go! We'll have a fantastic time.

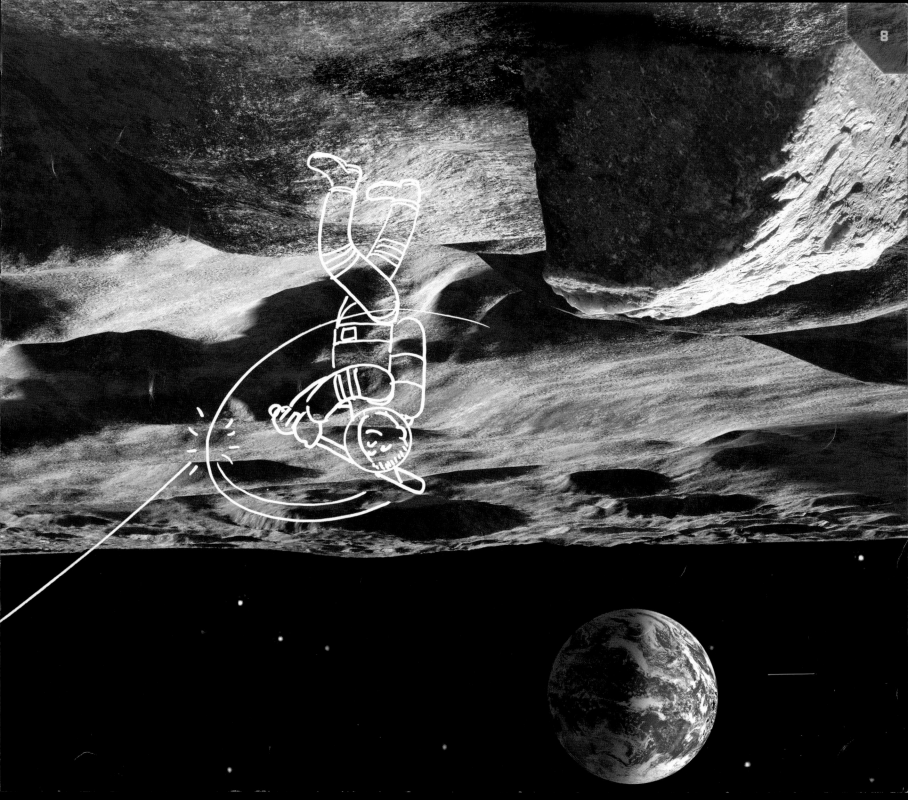

THE MOON

Dear Diary,
   Today I hit a baseball almost half a mile. I touched each base and made a home run before it hit the ground . . .

   As the spaceship approaches the Moon, my excitement mounts. I hurry to put on my space suit. It will keep me cool during the scorching day and provide me with air while I'm exploring. On Earth, the atmosphere acts like a blanket, keeping temperatures from getting too hot or too cold. But the Moon has no atmosphere. Temperatures rise above the boiling point of water during the day and fall far below freezing at night.

   After I leave the spaceship, the first things I notice are the craters. Some are bigger than a football field. Others are smaller than a penny. All around I see a dead world colored in shades of gray and tan. I examine a handful of moon dust that looks like kitchen scouring powder. Then I gather some rocks for souvenirs.

   Now it's time to have a little fun. I bound across the surface of the Moon like a kangaroo. I brought my favorite baseball, and it's time to give it a whack. WOW! On the Moon, I can hit a ball ten times farther than I can on Earth. Look out, Babe Ruth!

CONCLUSION: The Moon is too hot during the day and too cold at night. But it's a great place for sports!

FASCINATING FACTS: Footprints left by astronauts will remain for millions of years because the Moon has no wind and rain to wash them away.

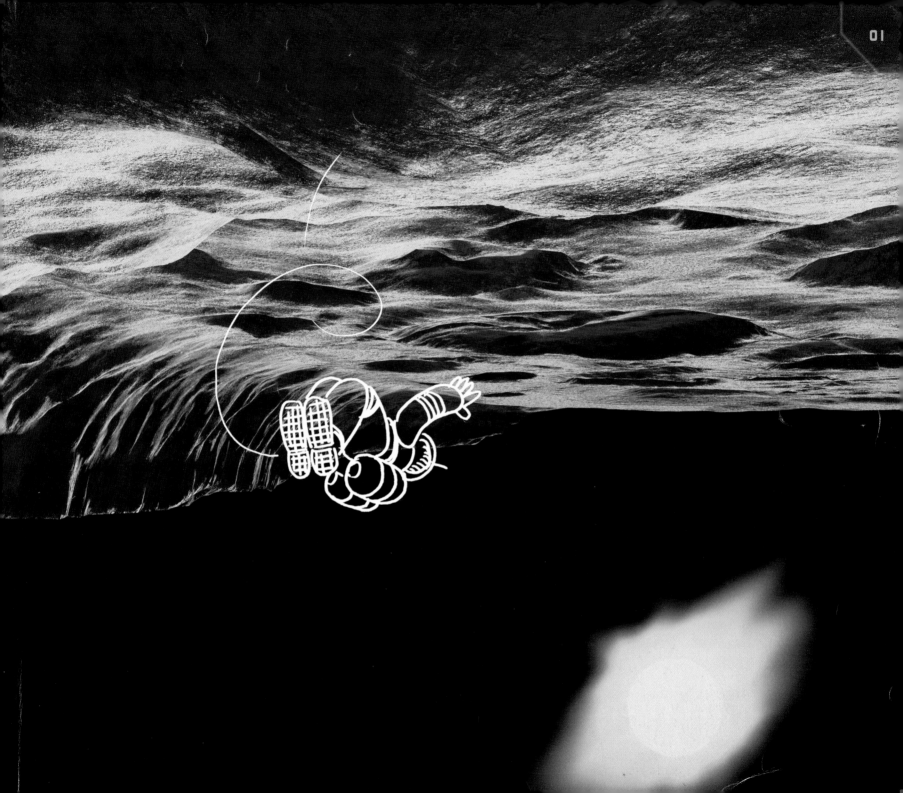

MERCURY

Dear Diary,

Today I played "catch up" with Mercury. Speedy Mercury zips around the sun six times faster than the space shuttle orbits Earth . . .

I arrive on Mercury in late afternoon. Above me, the Sun blazes fiercely in a black sky. It looks more than twice as big as it does from Earth. The ground is so hot I have to wear these steel mesh space boots.

The surface of Mercury is cracked and pocked with craters—big ones and little ones. Mercury looks a lot like the Moon. The gravity feels stronger here, but not as strong as it is on Earth. I jump and somersault twice before I hit the ground.

I make camp and wait a few Earth days to see what Mercury is like after dark. Soon the Sun sets. But just when I think night has arrived, the Sun does something amazing. It reverses direction and comes back up! I wait around until the Sun sets again—this time for good.

Now it's colder than December at the North Pole. Thousands of stars gleam like jewels in the black sky. Two bright stars catch my eye. One is blue green Earth, and the other is cream-colored Venus, my next stop.

CONCLUSION: To see the Sun act like a jack-in-the-box, visit Mercury.

FASCINATING FACTS: The atmosphere of Earth scatters the Sun's light and makes the sky appear blue. But Mercury has almost no atmosphere, and so the sky appears black, even in the daytime.

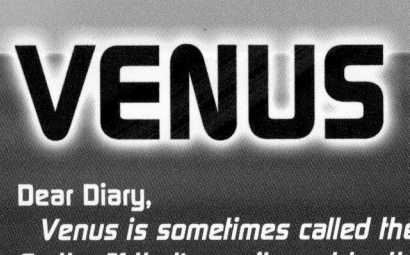

VENUS

Dear Diary,

Venus is sometimes called the "twin" of Earth. If that's so, it must be the evil twin . . .

On Earth, I've seen this sparkling planet in the evening sky, and now I can't wait to see it up close. After all, Venus is named for the Roman goddess of love and beauty.

But when I step onto the surface of the planet, I'm sorry I came. Venus isn't a pleasant place to be. In every direction, I see a terrible, red world. Imagine the hottest oven you can think of—Venus is even hotter. If I weren't wearing my suit I'd be burned to a crisp. And the atmosphere is so heavy that I feel like I'm walking underwater.

The air consists mostly of carbon dioxide, the same gas that makes soft drinks fizz. High above, thick clouds race across the sky, three times faster than a hurricane. I look up and think, "Maybe it will rain." But the clouds are made of a deadly acid, and any rain would probably burn a hole in my space suit.

Venus has traces of sulfur dioxide in its atmosphere. I fill my air sampler and take a sniff. Yuck! Venus smells like burned matches. And it's noisy too. Lightning flashes, and thunder rumbles now and then.

CONCLUSION: If you win an all-expense paid trip to Venus—don't go!

FASCINATING FACTS: The temperature on Venus is hot enough to melt lead. En route to the surface of Venus, a traveler would pass through clouds of sulfuric acid, hurricane-force winds, and lightning.

MARS

Dear Diary,

I went looking for Martians today—with a microscope...

I can't wait to visit Mars. Scientists say it's the planet most like Earth, and I'm hoping it's something like Hawaii. As my spaceship comes in for a landing, I spot sand dunes, deserts, and dried-up riverbeds below. The ship swoops over a huge volcano that's three times higher than Mount Everest.

When I step out onto the surface, I see that Mars looks like Earth's Death Valley. The ground is strewn with rocks and looks like a stony desert. The brown landscape stretches to the horizon, and the sky is a pinkish color. Mars has a thin, wispy atmosphere with icy winds that blow clouds of dust into the air. It's freezing cold. If I took off my space suit, I couldn't breathe the air and I'd also get a horrible sunburn.

Above me, I see Phobos, one of Mars's two moons. The other moon, Deimos, looks like a speck in the sky. I read my travel guide and discover that any life on Mars must be very tiny—if it exists at all. I hope I didn't accidentally squash anybody.

CONCLUSION: No animals, no people, no plants, no fun.

FASCINATING FACTS: Today, Mars is much colder and drier than Earth. But it may have been warmer and wetter in the past. Mars has the largest volcano we know of in the solar system. Some scientists believe that long ago, microbes might have evolved on Mars.

JUPITER

Dear Diary,
*If you want excitement and adventure,
you'll find it on Jupiter . . .*

I'm on my way to Jupiter. In front of me, bands of red, yellow, and orange clouds swirl around an enormous planet. A huge red spot that looks like the center of a target whirls into view. I'm headed straight toward it.

Jupiter is a giant ball of gas and liquid, and there's no solid surface to land on. So I've decided to plunge my spaceship through the rolling clouds—but not too far. Winds whip around with hurricane force, and the radiation could fry me to a cinder. If I could stand somewhere on this gas ball, I'd weigh more than twice as much as I weigh on Earth.

I enter the clouds. Suddenly a super-bolt of lightning strikes the ship. A thunderstorm rages around me. I sample the air and get a whiff of ammonia. Yikes! The ship is going down and down. Now the clouds are turning into a thick soup. I shine a flashlight out the portal and see ripples of something shiny and metallic. The pressure is so great that the hydrogen air has turned to liquid. I'd better blast off, while I still can.

CONCLUSION: Not for campers—no place to drive your tent stakes.

FASCINATING FACTS: It would take 1,300 planets the size of Earth to fill up one Jupiter-sized candy bowl. The Great Red Spot, a hurricane-like storm, wider across than three planet Earths, has been raging for more than 300 years.

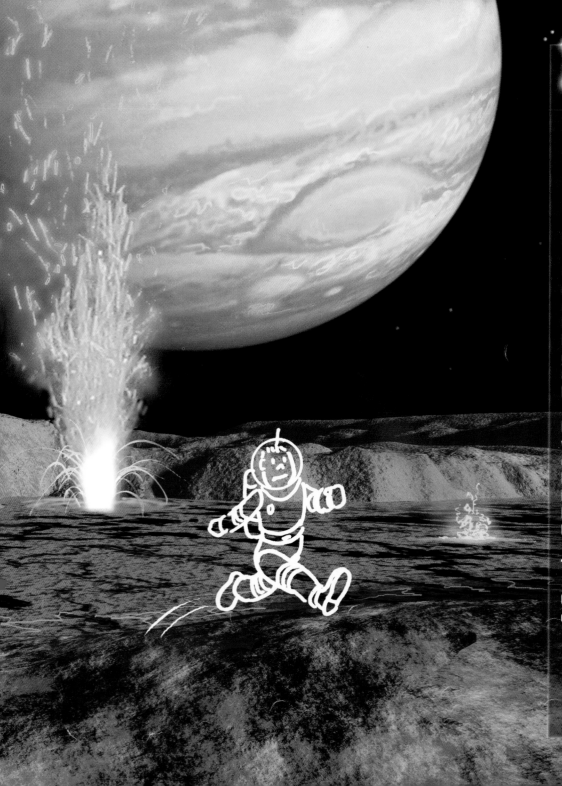

IO

Dear Diary,

From space, Io looks like a pizza with extra cheese, olives, and tomatoes . . .

I've made a side trip to Io, one of Jupiter's moons. The first thing I notice is that Io's surface is ablaze with color. Even the atmosphere is colorful—eerie flashes of blue, green, and red flicker on the horizon.

Standing on Io is an awesome experience. Frequent Io-quakes make the ground shudder. Volcanoes shoot gas and molten rock into the air. As the sulfur gas rises into the atmosphere, it starts to freeze and fall to the ground. To my right, I see a field of this yellow "snow," marked with streaks of green and spots of bright red. To my left, a lava lake bubbles and sizzles.

Above me, Jupiter blots out a big chunk of the sky. Io is caught in a gravitational tug-of-war between giant Jupiter and two of Jupiter's other moons, Europa and Ganymede. This tugging causes material inside Io to reach high temperatures until it comes spewing out. But away from the volcanoes, Io's surface is bitterly cold.

Uh oh! A vent just opened up near me. Time to leave!

CONCLUSION: There's never a boring day on Io.

FASCINATING FACTS: Io is the innermost of Jupiter's four largest moons. Io's volcanoes spew plumes of sulfur and sulfur dioxide that turn different colors as they fall to the ground. The *Galileo* spacecraft spotted auroras, similar to Earth's northern lights, in Io's atmosphere.

SATURN

Dear Diary,

Today I rode the solar system's weirdest merry-go-round . . .

Jupiter and Io are exciting, but Saturn wins the beauty contest. In front of me is a huge world covered in a golden haze. Here and there white clouds billow up from below. From a distance, the rings circling the planet look smooth and solid. But as I get closer, I see that each ring is made up of chunks of ice and rock—some the size of sugar grains, others bigger than barns.

I'm ready for a little fun, so I gently ease my ship downward. From this angle, the rings look like a giant ice-skating rink. I can't really skate here, but I can go play in the snow. I open the hatch, fire up my jet pack, and take off. Ice particles bounce off my suit. An icy boulder heaves into view, and the two of us travel together. I feel like a human satellite swirling around this mighty planet.

The Sun is a small beacon in the distance. Around me, ice crystals sparkle in the dim light. I'm a billion miles from home, riding the rings of Saturn in outer space.

Time to head back to the spaceship. I'll never forget this fantastic day!

CONCLUSION: Saturn is a great place for a snowball fight.

FASCINATING FACTS: Saturn is the second-largest planet in the solar system. Other planets have rings, but Saturn's rings are the most spectacular. Small moons orbit within Saturn's ring system.

ENCELADUS

Dear Diary,

From space Saturn's mini-moon Enceladus looks like a giant snowball . . .

Since I couldn't actually land on Saturn, I'll visit two of the gas planet's moons instead. The first stop is Enceladus, one of the brightest, whitest objects in the solar system.

After landing near Enceladus's south pole, I hike across an icy field strewn with rocks and boulders. Everywhere the ground is cracked and folded. Like Io, Enceladus has been squeezed and stretched by the gravity of Saturn and two of its moons.

Enceladus is one of the coldest places in the Saturn system. But it's actually warmer at the south pole than it is at the equator. Imagine if that happened on Earth. Then Antarctica would be warmer than the Sahara!

WOW! A geyser just erupted on my right, spewing water and ice miles into the sky. The spray jetted up from one of the cracks— like a cold version of Old Faithful in Earth's Yellowstone Park. WHOOSH! There goes another one. A pool of water must exist just below the surface of Enceladus. And if there's water, there could be tiny creatures swimming around down there. I wish I had time to do some ice fishing and find out.

CONCLUSION: If you want to open a snow cone stand, visit Enceladus.

FASCINATING FACT: The *Cassini* spacecraft spotted geysers as it flew by Enceladus. Scientists believe that the mix of liquid water and organic molecules found on Enceladus make it a good place to search for possible life.

TITAN

Dear Diary,
It's a lazy, hazy day on Titan . . .

I'm heading toward Saturn's largest moon, Titan. From space, this mysterious world is hidden by dense fog, and I'm not sure what I'll find when I get there. A few hours later, I land, open the hatch, and climb out.

Around me is a strange, spooky landscape. Everything looks orange, even the sky. This haze in the air isn't fog—it's smog. A good day on Titan is worse than the smoggiest day in the smoggiest city on Earth.

In the distance, I see ridges and peaks— and a pool with an island in the middle. But that pool isn't water. It's liquid methane, and I'd become an instant ice cube if I took a dip.

I sample the atmosphere and see that it's mostly nitrogen, just like Earth's. Oh no, it's started to rain. But this methane shower won't bring May flowers—not at -260° F (-162° C).

The ground gives a little as I walk, like loose sand. Pebbles coated with orange dust are scattered around. I look closer and see that they are actually chunks of ice. It's so cold here that the ice is as strong as granite.

CONCLUSION: For a Halloween landscape that's out of this world, visit Titan!

FASCINATING FACTS: Of all the moons in the solar system, only Saturn's moon Titan has a thick atmosphere. Scientists believe that Titan's atmosphere is similar to that of Earth four billion years ago. The building blocks of life might also be present on Titan.

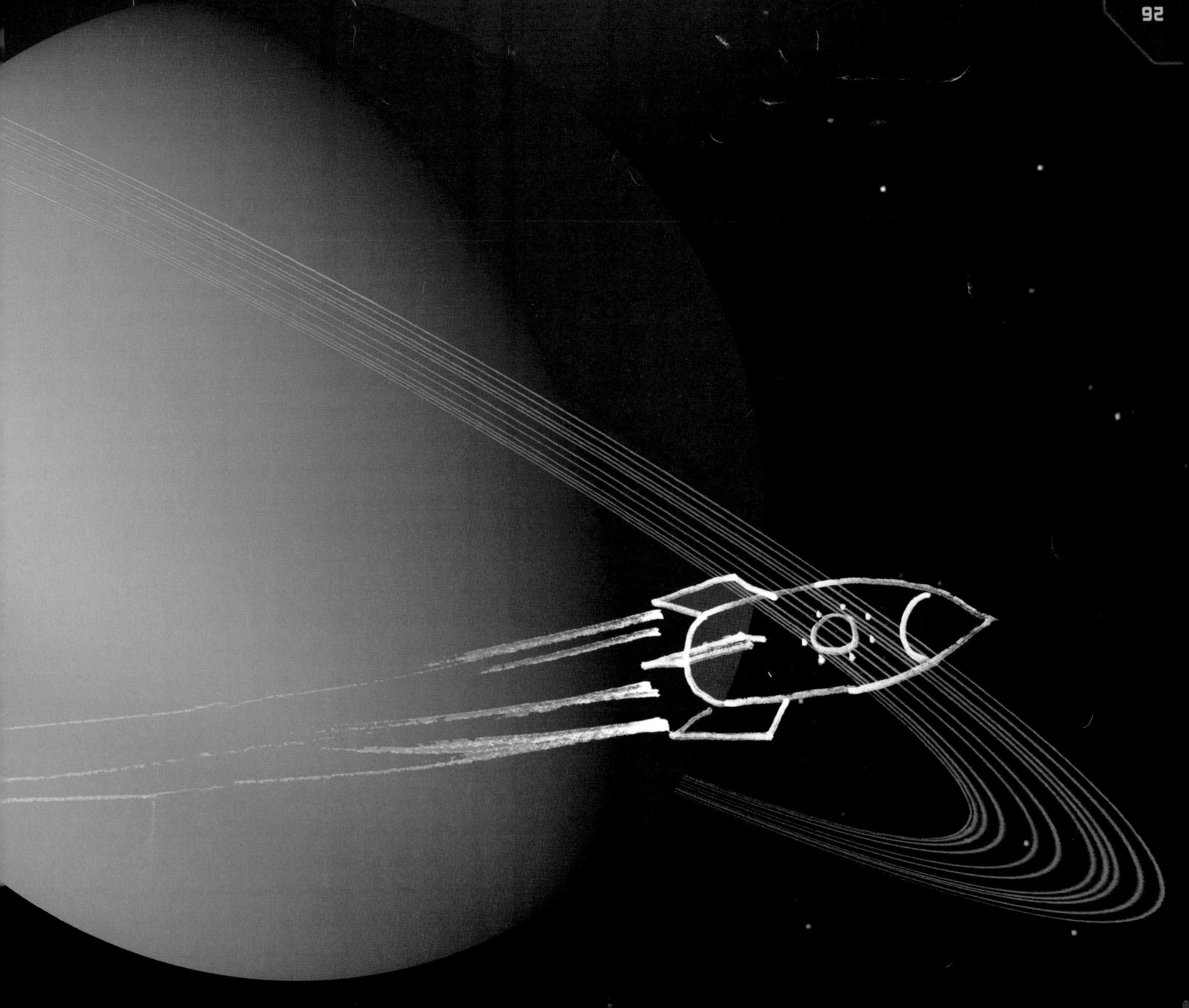

URANUS

Dear Diary,

Just got a radio message from Mom. She reminded me to take out the trash . . .

I'm in orbit around Uranus—one crazy planet. It rolls around the Sun on its side. What can you do with a planet like that?

After analyzing the atmosphere, I discover that Uranus is just another oversized gas ball—an icy world covered with clouds of hydrogen, helium, and methane. Uranus looks smooth and bland from space. But now that I'm closer, I see faint patterns in the clouds, 11 thin rings, and about 20 moons. The pale blue green color makes me homesick for my own blue planet, Earth.

I think I'll stay indoors today and do a little housekeeping. Tomorrow I'm heading for Neptune, and I have to get ready. I need to replace the Velcro that keeps my meal tray in place. Last night, the macaroni and cheese floated off and ended up stuck to the instrument panel. One of the solar panels was hit by a meteor, and I have to repair it. And it's time to recycle the trash and update the ship's log. Even we daring space explorers have chores to do.

CONCLUSION: Food in free fall is far from funny.

FASCINATING FACTS: The atmosphere of Uranus, like that of Jupiter and Saturn, would be poisonous to breathe. Uranus is tilted on one side. This may have been caused by a possible collision between Uranus and a planet-sized object.

NEPTUNE

Dear Diary,

Today's weather report—windy with patches of diamonds . . .

I gaze out the window at beautiful blue Neptune, the outermost of the gas giant planets, and my last stop before heading home. I see a few feathery clouds that look similar to clouds on Earth. But Neptune's atmosphere is made up of hydrogen, helium, and methane like that of Uranus. Anyone who breathed it would die.

As I descend into the clouds, the spaceship is tossed about like a cork in a typhoon. Neptune has the wildest weather I've seen yet. The winds are gusting at 1,200 miles (1,930 kilometers) per hour—three times stronger than those on Jupiter.

As I fall through the clouds, the atmosphere becomes as thick as pudding. I'm floating in a muck of molten rock, water, liquid ammonia, and methane. Suddenly, something slams into the spaceship. Whoa! Could it be . . . ? Some scientists say the intense heat and pressure in Neptune's atmosphere may create basketball-size diamonds that rain down on the planet. It sure would be fun to shovel the walk after that kind of storm!

CONCLUSION: Neptune is a "gem" of a planet.

FASCINATING FACTS: The methane in Neptune's atmosphere produces its blue color. Scientists have discovered that heating and squeezing methane in a lab creates diamonds. Some astronomers think that Neptune's (and Uranus's) lower atmosphere might contain trillions of large diamonds.

EARTH

Dear Diary,

I can't wait to breathe Earth's warm air . . .

I've had enough. I'm suddenly homesick for my home planet. I could blast off for Pluto, but they say it's just another icy world—lifeless, cold, and dark. So I'm heading home.

There it is! There's Earth, hanging in space like a Christmas tree ornament. I can see its blue oceans covered with swirls of white clouds.

I've visited some wonderful worlds and seen incredible sights—from topsy-turvy Uranus to golden Saturn—from scorching Venus to freezing Enceladus. But nothing is as beautiful as Earth—home to lilies and ladybugs, sunflowers, and songbirds.

My spaceship zooms over forests and jungles. I see children playing in a meadow. Nowhere in the solar system did I find anything as amazing as an oak tree or as delicate as a spiderweb. Nowhere else could a human live without bringing along gifts from our precious planet—water, food, and a bubble of air. I'm finally back where I belong.

What did I find out? Earth is neither too hot nor too cold, too big nor too small. It's just right for life. I guess we'll have to learn to take care of it. It's the only home we have.

CONCLUSION: It's great to be home!

FASCINATING FACTS: More than 70 percent of Earth's surface is covered with liquid water. It's the only planet in the solar system that's teeming with plant, animal, and human life.

SOLAR SYSTEM FACTS

THE MOON

SIZE: About one-fourth the size, or diameter, of Earth

GRAVITY: A 60-pound (27-kilogram) kid would weigh 10 pounds (4.5 kilograms) on the Moon.

MOON'S DAY: The Moon requires 27.5 Earth days to rotate, or spin, once on its axis.

MOON'S ORBIT: The Moon revolves, or moves, around Earth once every 27.5 days. Both the Moon and Earth revolve around the Sun every 365 days.

ATMOSPHERE: None

TEMPERATURE: Daytime: 265°F (130°C); Nighttime: -170°F (-112°C)

SPACECRAFT VISITING THE MOON: *Luna 1* through *24* (USSR/Russia); *Ranger 4* through *9* (USA); *Surveyor 1* through *7* (USA); *Apollo 8* through *17* (USA); and many others.

MERCURY

SIZE: About one-third the diameter of Earth

GRAVITY: A 60-pound (27-kilogram) kid would weigh about 23 pounds (10 kilograms) on Mercury.

MERCURY'S DAY: Mercury requires 59 Earth days to rotate on its axis.

MERCURY'S YEAR: Mercury requires 88 Earth days to revolve once around the Sun.

ATMOSPHERE: Very thin—made mostly of sodium and helium with smaller amounts of oxygen, potassium, and hydrogen

TEMPERATURE: From 800°F (427°C) during the day to -298°F (-183°C) at night

SPACECRAFT VISITING MERCURY: *Mariner 2* and *Mariner 10* (USA); *Messenger* (USA)

VENUS

SIZE: Slightly smaller than Earth—95 percent of Earth's diameter

GRAVITY: A 60-pound (27-kilogram) kid would weigh about 54 pounds (24 kilograms) on Venus.

VENUS'S DAY: Venus requires 243 Earth days to rotate once on its axis.

VENUS'S YEAR: Venus requires 225 Earth days to revolve once around the Sun.

ATMOSPHERE: Very thick—made up mostly of carbon dioxide. High clouds on Venus contain droplets of sulfuric acid.

TEMPERATURE: The daytime temperature is 872°F (468°C) and it doesn't cool down much at night.

SPACECRAFT VISITING VENUS: *Venera 1* through *16* (USSR/Russia); *Zond 2* (USSR/Russia); *Mariner 2, Mariner 10* (USA); *Pioneer Venus 1, Pioneer Venus 2* (USA); *Vega 1, Vega 2* (USSR/Russia); *Magellan 4* (USA); *Galileo* (USA)

MARS

SIZE: A little more than half the diameter of Earth

GRAVITY: A 60-pound (27-kilogram) kid would weigh about 23 pounds (10 kilograms) on Mars.

MARS'S DAY: Mars requires 24½ Earth hours to rotate on its axis.

MARS'S YEAR: Mars requires 687 Earth days to revolve once around the Sun.

ATMOSPHERE: Mostly carbon dioxide

TEMPERATURE: The average temperature on Mars is -81°F (-63°C)

SPACECRAFT VISITING MARS: *Mars 1* through *7* (USSR/Russia); *Mariner 3* and *4, 6, 7, 8,* and *9* (USA); *Viking 1* and *2* (USA); *Mars Global Surveyor* (USA); *Pathfinder* (USA); *Mars Climate Orbiter* (USA); *Mars Polar Lander/Deep Space 2* (USA); *Mars Exploration Rovers* (USA); *Exploration Rovers* (USA); *Mars Express Orbiter* (European Space Agency); *Mars Reconnaissance Orbiter* (USA); and others

JUPITER

SIZE: More than 11 times the diameter of Earth

GRAVITY: A 60-pound kid (27-kilogram) would weigh about 142 pounds (64 kilograms) on Jupiter.

JUPITER'S DAY: Jupiter requires 10 Earth hours to rotate once on its axis.

JUPITER'S YEAR: Jupiter requires 11.8 Earth years to revolve once around the Sun

ATMOSPHERE: Mostly hydrogen and helium

TEMPERATURE: The temperature at the core of the planet is almost 55,000°F (30,000°C) The cloud-top temperature averages -244°F (-153°C).

SPACECRAFT VISITING JUPITER: *Pioneer 10* and *11* (USA); *Voyager 1* and *2* (USA); *Galileo* (USA); *Ulysses* (European Space Agency)

IO

SIZE: About the diameter of Earth's Moon

GRAVITY: A 60-pound kid (27-kilogram) would weigh about 11 pounds (5 kilograms) on Io.

IO'S DAY: Io requires 42 Earth hours to rotate once on its axis.

IO'S ORBIT: Io orbits Jupiter every 42 hours.

ATMOSPHERE: Very thin atmosphere of sulfur dioxide

TEMPERATURE: From 2,000°F (1,093°C) near a volcano to -260°F (-162°C)

SPACECRAFT VISITING IO: *Pioneer 10* and *11* (USA); *Voyager 1* and *2* (USA); *Galileo* (USA)

SATURN

SIZE: Nine times Earth's diameter, not counting the rings

GRAVITY: A 60-pound kid (27-kilogram) would weigh about 64 pounds (29 kilograms) on Saturn.

SATURN'S DAY: Saturn requires 10 Earth hours and 14 minutes to rotate once on its axis.

SATURN'S YEAR: Saturn requires 29.5 Earth years to revolve once around the Sun.

ATMOSPHERE: Mostly hydrogen with some helium, methane, and ammonia

TEMPERATURE: The temperature of the cloud tops is -308°F (-189°C). Temperatures become very hot at lower altitudes.

SPACECRAFT VISITING SATURN: *Pioneer 11* (USA); *Voyager 1* and *2* (USA); *Cassini* (International)

ENCELADUS

SIZE: About 15 percent of the diameter of Earth's Moon

GRAVITY: A 60-pound (27-kilogram) kid would weigh about one-half pound (.22 kilograms) on Enceladus.

ENCELADUS'S DAY: Enceladus requires 1.4 days to rotate once on its axis.

ENCELADUS'S ORBIT: Enceladus orbits Saturn every 1.4 days.

ATMOSPHERE: About 91 percent water vapor with some nitrogen, carbon dioxide, and other molecules

TEMPERATURE: In most places, the temperatures average about -330°F (-201°C). At the south pole, the temperature is about -261°F (-163°C).

SPACECRAFT VISITING ENCELADUS: *Cassini* (International)

TITAN

SIZE: One and a half times bigger in diameter than Earth's Moon

GRAVITY: A 60-pound kid (27-kilogram) would weigh about 8.3 pounds (3.8 kilograms) on Titan.

TITAN'S DAY: Titan requires 16 Earth days to rotate once on its axis.

TITAN'S ORBIT: Titan orbits Saturn every 16 days.

ATMOSPHERE: Mostly nitrogen with some methane, ammonia, argon, and other compounds

TEMPERATURE: Temperatures average -290°F (-179°C)

SPACECRAFT VISITING TITAN: *Pioneer 11* (USA); *Voyager 1* and *2* (USA); *Cassini*-*Huygens* (International)

URANUS

SIZE: Four times the diameter of Earth

GRAVITY: A 60-pound kid (27-kilogram) would weigh about 53 pounds (24 kilograms) on Uranus.

URANUS'S DAY: Uranus requires 17 Earth hours and 14 minutes to rotate once on its axis.

URANUS'S YEAR: Uranus requires 84 Earth years to revolve once around the Sun.

ATMOSPHERE: Mostly hydrogen with some helium and methane

TEMPERATURE: At its surface, the temperature on Uranus is about -323°F (-197°C). Temperatures rise and become quite hot at lower altitudes.

SPACECRAFT VISITING URANUS: *Voyager 2* (USA)

NEPTUNE

SIZE: Almost four times the diameter of Earth

GRAVITY: A 60-pound kid (27-kilogram) would weigh 67 pounds (30 kilograms) on Neptune.

NEPTUNE'S DAY: Neptune requires about 16 Earth hours to rotate once on its axis.

NEPTUNE'S YEAR: Neptune requires 165 Earth years to revolve once around the Sun.

ATMOSPHERE: Mostly hydrogen with some helium and methane

TEMPERATURE: The cloud-top temperature is about -328°F (-200°C). Temperatures become very hot at lower altitudes.

SPACECRAFT VISITING NEPTUNE: *Voyager 2* (USA)

EARTH

SIZE: The diameter of Earth is 7,909 miles (12,728 kilometers).

GRAVITY: A 60-pound kid (27-kilogram) would weigh 60 pounds (27 kilograms) on Earth.

EARTH'S DAY: Earth rotates on its axis once every 24 hours.

EARTH'S ORBIT: Earth revolves around the Sun every 365 days.

ATMOSPHERE: Earth's atmosphere is composed of 78 percent nitrogen, 21 percent oxygen, and 1 percent other gases, including carbon dioxide and argon.

TEMPERATURE: Temperatures on Earth range from 136°F (58 °C) to -129°F (-89°C).

SPACECRAFT ORBITING THE EARTH: *Sputnik 1* and *2* (USSR/Russia); *Explorer 1* (USA); *Vanguard 1* (USA); *Hubble Space Telescope* (USA); and many others

GLOSSARY

atmosphere: the envelope of gas or air surrounding a planet or moon

ammonia: a strong-smelling gas made of nitrogen and hydrogen

craters: pits in the ground blasted out by falling meteorites

day: the amount of time it takes for a planet or moon to make one complete turn on its axis

gravity: the force that draws objects toward one another

helium: a very light gas; one of the chemical elements

hydrogen: a colorless, flammable gas; the lightest chemical element

methane: a colorless, odorless gas, sometimes used as a fuel on Earth

microbes: tiny organisms that can be observed only through a microscope

molten: melted or made into a liquid by heat

nitrogen: a colorless, odorless gas that forms four-fifths of the Earth's atmosphere

orbit: to travel in a closed path around the Sun or a planet

planetary year: the amount of time it takes for a planet along with its moons to revolve around the Sun

radiation: intense energy consisting of penetrating sub-atomic particles or electromagnetic waves, which include x-rays, light waves, radio waves, and others

revolve: to move around a point, such as the Sun or a planet, in an orbit

rotation: the movement of a planet or moon as it turns on its axis

solar system: the Sun and its family of planets, moons, comets, and asteroids

sodium: a chemical element usually found in a combined form

sulfur: a pale yellow chemical element

WEBSITES FOR KIDS

Kids Astronomy
http://www.kidsastronomy.com/
Information on the solar system, galaxies, black holes, quasars, plus games, puzzles, and space jokes

NASA Kids
http://kids.msfc.nasa.gov/
Activities, games, and information about NASA, rocket science, Earth, seasons, the space shuttle, space and beyond, and many other topics

Solar System Simulator
http://space.jpl.nasa.gov/
This simulator shows a specified object in the solar system as it would appear from a spacecraft, a planet, or a moon on a particular day

The Space Place
http://spaceplace.jpl.nasa.gov/index.shtml
Spacecrafts, space facts, play Space Trivia, or go on a Mars adventure, plus much more

Zoom Astronomy
http://www.enchantedlearning.com/subjects/astronomy/toc.shtml
All about the solar system, a tutorial, crafts, coloring pages, puzzles, quizzes, your weight on other worlds, and much more

BOOKS FOR KIDS

Croswell, Ken. *Ten Worlds: Everything That Orbits the Sun.* Honesdale, PA: Boyds Mills Press, 2006.

Herschmann, Kris. *Space and the Planets.* Magic School Bus Chapter series. New York: Scholastic, 2003.

Kerrod, Robin. *Planet Library series* (10 Volumes). Minneapolis: Lerner Publications Company, 2000.

O'Shaughnessy, Tam E., and Sally Ride. *Exploring Our Solar System.* New York: Crown Books for Young Readers, 2003.

Simon, Seymour. *Our Solar System.* New York: William Morrow, 1992.

Tanton, Linda Elkins. *Jupiter and Saturn.* New York: Facts on File, 2006.

Tanton, Linda Elkins. *The Sun, Mercury, and Venus.* New York: Facts on File, 2006.

Tanton, Linda Elkins. *Uranus, Neptune, Pluto, and the Outer Planets.* New York: Facts on File, 2006.

ACKNOWLEDGMENTS

I'd like to thank Fred Marschak, astronomy instructor at Santa Barbara Community College for his considerable help and Dr. Gregory L. Vogt, who gave me invaluable advice and double-checked my facts and figures. I also wish to express my deep gratitude to Dr. Stan Peale, professor emeritus of physics at the University of California at Santa Barbara who read and corrected an early draft and patiently answered my many questions. Dr. Ann Sprague and Dr. Larry Lebofsky, both of the University of Arizona, also commented on this manuscript.

BIBLIOGRAPHY

Books

Benson, Michael. *Beyond: Visions of the Interplanetary Probes.* New York: Harry N. Abrams, 2003.

Hodge, Paul. *Higher Than Everest: An Adventurer's Guide to the Solar System.* Cambridge: Cambridge University Press, 2001.

Pasachoff, Jay M., and Alex Filippenko. *The Cosmos: Astronomy in the New Millennium.* Pacific Grove, CA: Brooks/Cole-Thomson Learning, 2004.

"New Light on the Solar System." (special issue) *Scientific American,* Inc., 2003.

Sparrow, Giles. *The Solar System: Exploring the Planets and Their Moons, from Mercury to Pluto and Beyond.* San Diego, CA: Thunder Bay Press, 2006.

Stern, S. Alan. *Worlds Beyond: The Thrill of Planetary Exploration As Told By Leading Experts.* New York and London: Cambridge University Press, 2003.

Taylor, F. W. *The Cambridge Photographic Guide to the Planets.* London: Cambridge University Press, 2002.

Websites

Jet Propulsion Laboratory
http://www.jpl.nasa.gov/
Latest statistics and information about the planets and moons

NASA
http://spacelink.nasa.gov/NASA.Projects/.index.html
Complete information about current NASA projects

NASA Kids
http://kids.msfc.nasa.gov/
Kid-friendly explanations of astronomical phenomena